女声合唱とピアノのための

この星の上で

谷川俊太郎＝作詩
松下　耕＝作曲

On our Planet
for female choir and piano

Words by Shuntaro TANIKAWA
Composed by Ko MATSUSHITA

カワイ出版

女声合唱とピアノのための
この星の上で

　いままで、たくさんの作品を出版していただきました。

　そして、そのたびに、この《巻頭言》というか、《序文》を書いてきました。

　今回、この作品について、なにか語らなければいけない、そう思えば思うほど、私は言葉を失います。

　この曲に対しての、私からのコメントは、何もありません。ただただ、谷川さんの詩の世界に感動し、寄り添いながら、作曲させていただいた、とだけ、申し上げます。

　ですから（これは、近頃の私の作品に共通することなのですが）、すべての曲は、谷川さんの作品の一字一句たりとも省略、訂正しておりません。私なりの、詩に対する敬意です。

　《はる》は、この曲の冒頭に、ピアノ伴奏付きの曲として演奏されますが、この本の最後に同じ曲の無伴奏の版を載録しました。プログラムには組み込まず、《今年》を最終曲として演奏し、アンコールピースとして演奏していただく方法が、スマートではなかろうか、と思っています。

　この曲は組曲ですが、一曲、あるいは数曲を抜粋して演奏していただいても構いません。

2006 年 6 月

松下　耕

for female choir and piano

On our Planet

First of all, I would like to express my appreciation for "edition KAWAI" for their offer of sending many of my works to the public.

For every one of them, I wrote a few words for as 'Forewords' or 'Introduction'.

For this album, however, I could hardly find the proper words for all my utmost effort.

As a result, I decided not to write anything about this composition. I can only say that I was deeply impressed by Mr. Shuntaro Tanikawa's poems and tried to compose by simply expressing my total involvement with their world.

Therefore, as I do in all my recent compositions, not a single word is omitted or altered from Mr. Tanikawa's original as homage to the poems.

The song **"Halu (Spring)"** is to be performed at the beginning with the piano accompaniment, but the score without the accompaniment is included at the end of the book. I think it would be nice to sing it as an encore piece, after ending the program with **"Kotoshi (This Year)"**.

This composition is actually a suit, but you may choose one or a few pieces for your performance.

June, 2006
Ko MATSUSHITA
Translated by Fumiko ISHII

目次／Contents

この星の上で

		演奏時間	
はる （Spring）	……………………………………	（ca.2'20"）	…5
地球の客 （Guests of the Earth）	……………………	（ca.4'00"）	…12
おべんとうの歌 （A Song of Lunch）	……………	（ca.6'50"）	…22
ほほえみ （Smile）	…………………………………	（ca.3'45"）	…42
今年 （This Year）	…………………………………	（ca.6'10"）	…50

☆　☆　☆

はる〔無伴奏版〕（Spring〔A cappella version〕）	…………	（ca.2'50"）	…66
歌　詩（Text）	………………………………………………		…69

● 全曲の演奏時間＝約 26 分

《初演データ／Data》
● 委　嘱：国立音楽大学附属高等学校合唱部
　 初　演：2005 年 3 月 24 日
　　　　　オリンピック記念青少年センターホール
　　　　　《創部 10 周年記念　特別演奏会》
　　　　　指　揮　荒木泰俊
　　　　　ピアノ　星野安彦

● Commission : Kunitachi College Of Music
　　　　　　　 Affiliated High School Chorus
　 Premier Performance : 24th March 2005
　 National Institution for Youth Education Concert Hall
　 《The 10th Anniversary Special Concert》
　 Conductor : Yasutoshi ARAKI
　 Pianist : Yasuhiko HOSHINO

携帯サイトはこちら▶

出版情報＆ショッピング　カワイ出版ONLINE　https://www.editionkawai.jp/

はる

Halu
Spring

谷川俊太郎 作詩
Words by Shuntaro TANIKAWA
松下　耕 作曲
Composed by Ko MATSUSHITA

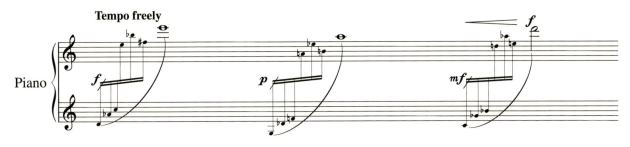

© Copyright 2006 by edition KAWAI, Tokyo, Japan. International Copyright Secured, All Rights Reserved.

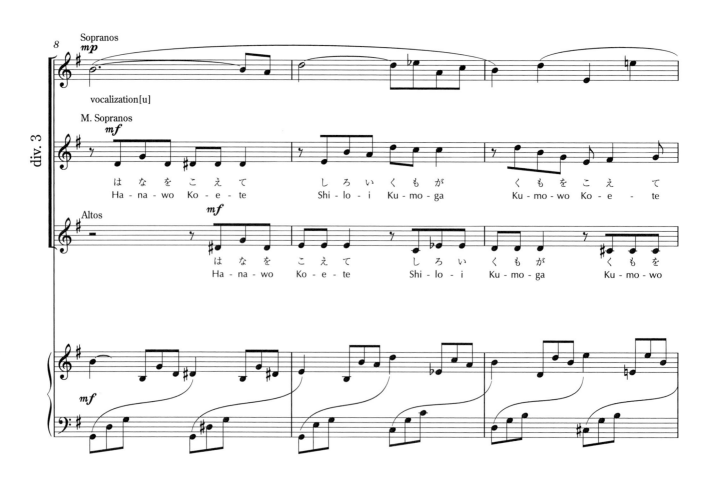

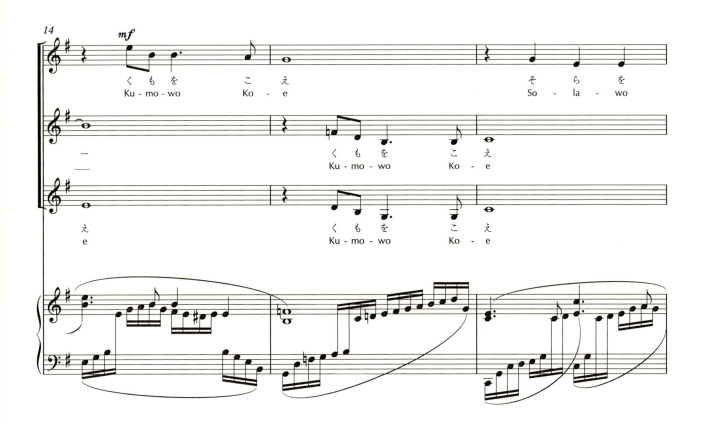

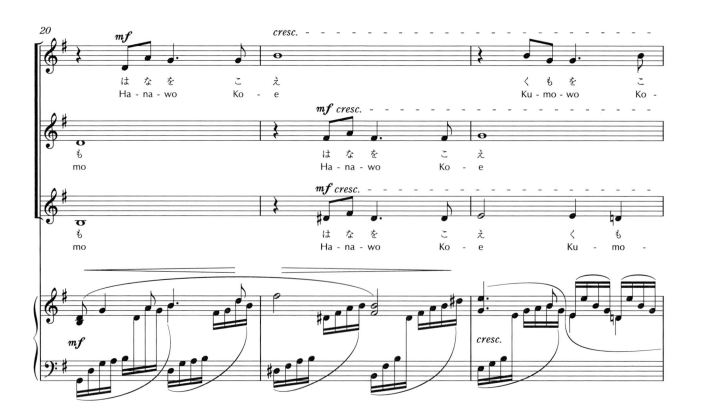

地球の客
Chikyu no Kyaku
Guests of the Earth

谷川俊太郎 作詩
Words by Shuntaro TANIKAWA
松下　耕 作曲
Composed by Ko MATSUSHITA

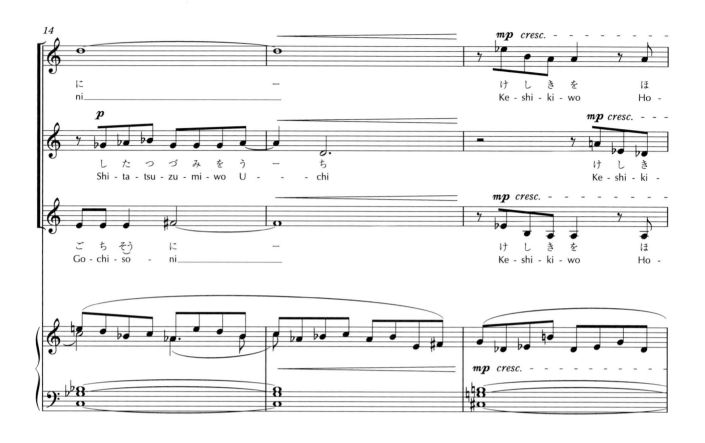

16

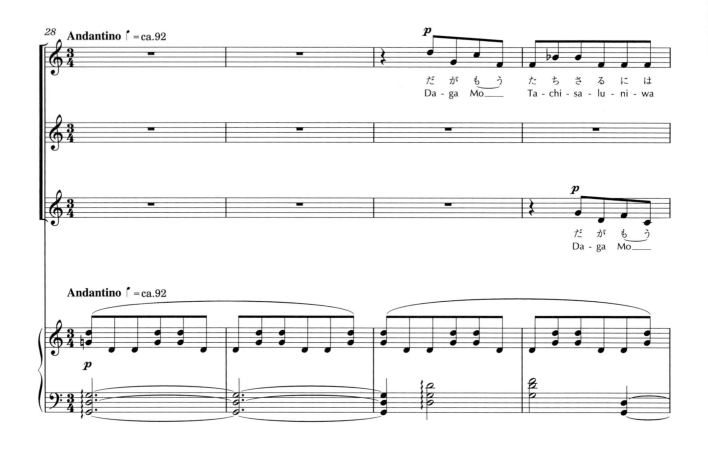

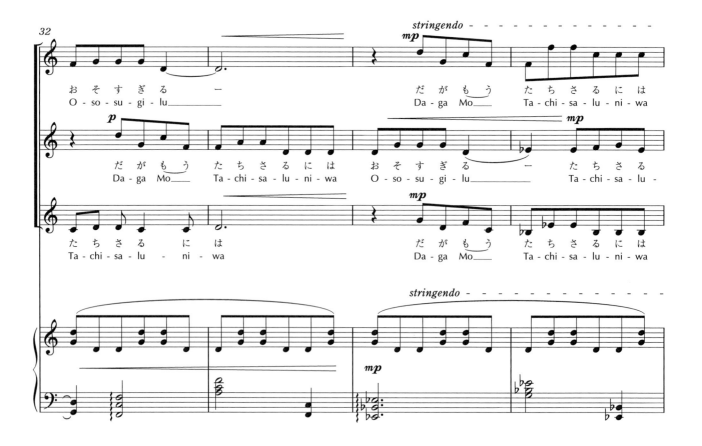

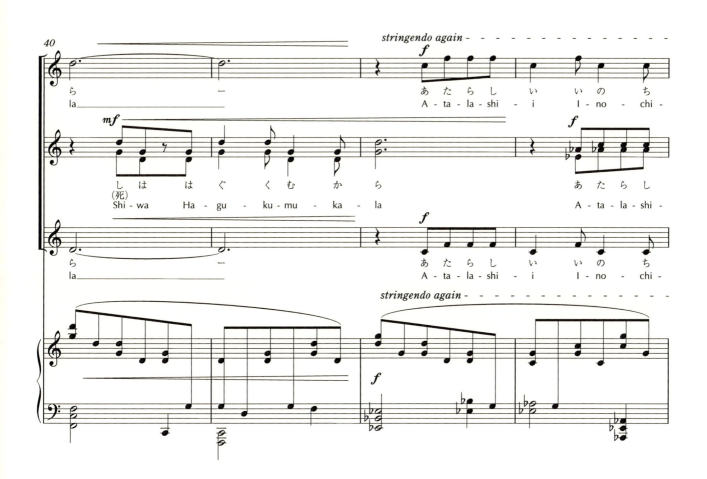

18

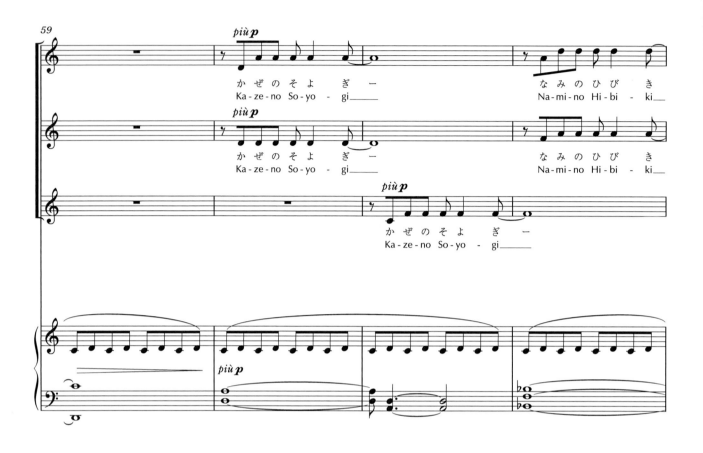

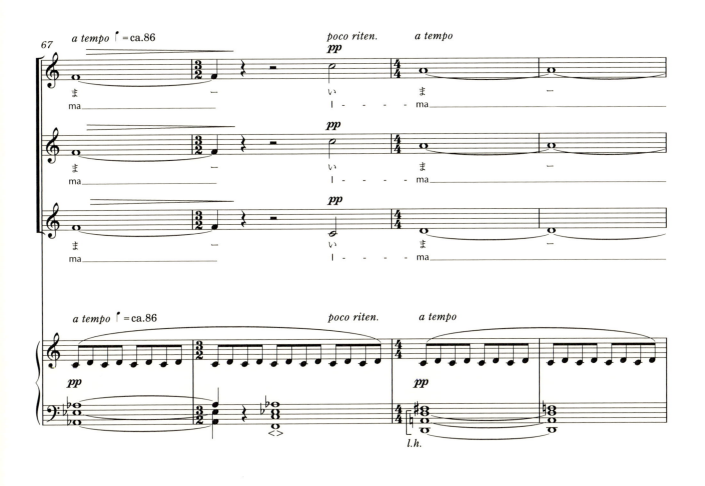
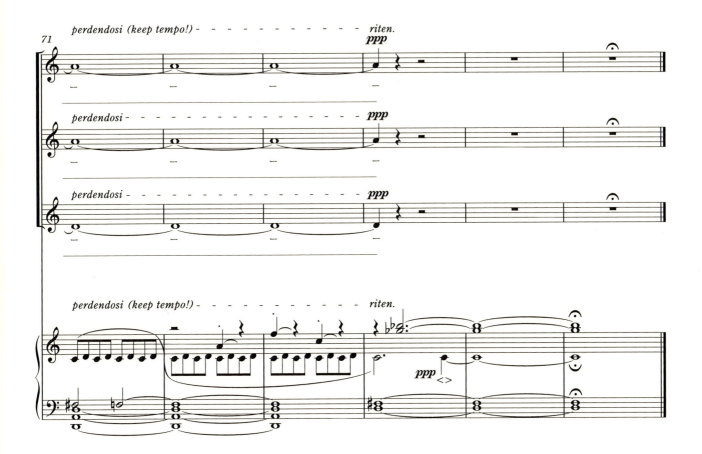

おべんとうの歌

Obento no Uta

A Song of Lunch

谷川俊太郎 作詩
Words by Shuntaro TANIKAWA
松下　耕 作曲
Composed by Ko MATSUSHITA

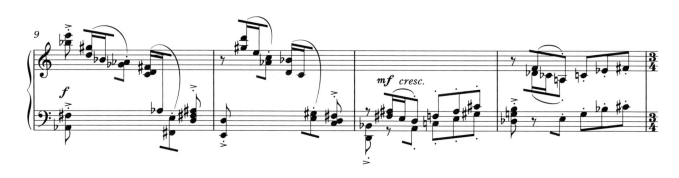

© Copyright 2006 by edition KAWAI, Tokyo, Japan. International Copyright Secured, All Rights Reserved.

楽譜・音楽書等出版物を複写・複製することは法律により禁じられております。

24

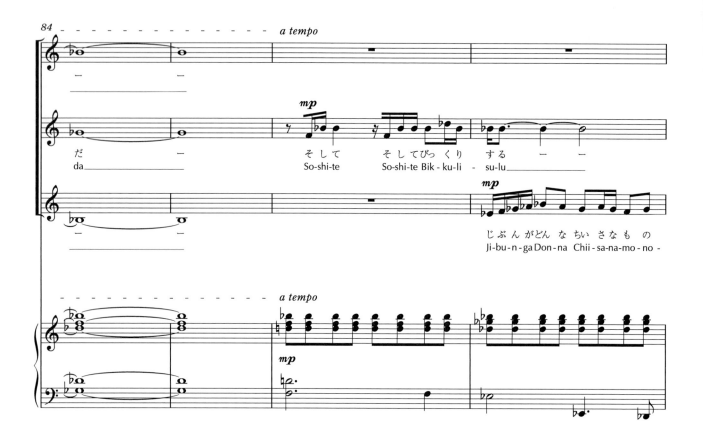

36

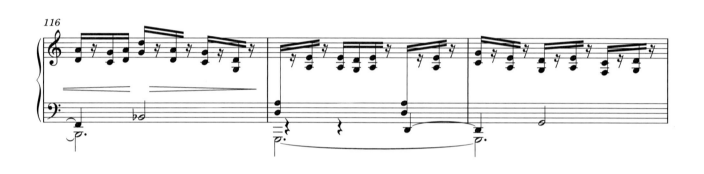

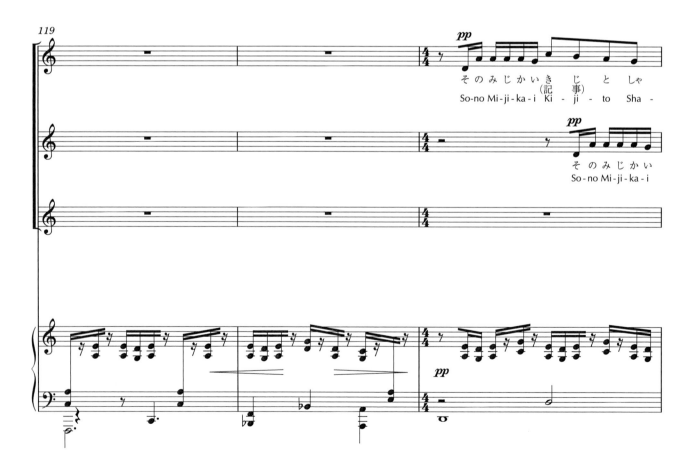

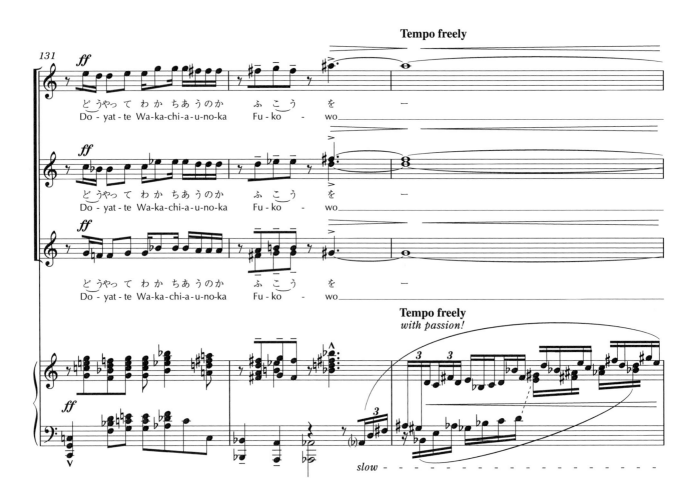

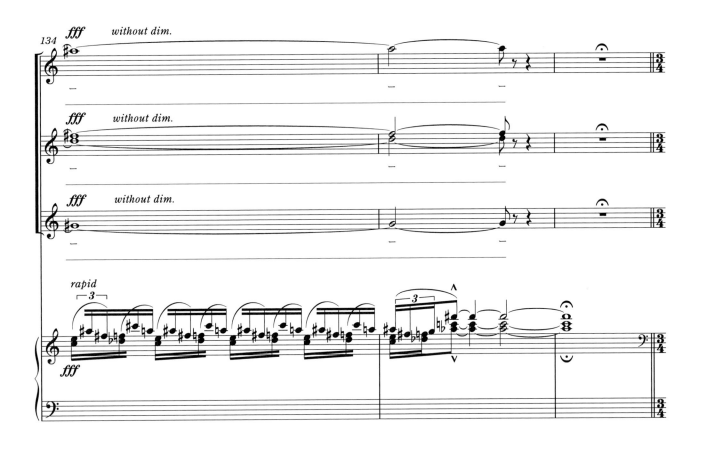

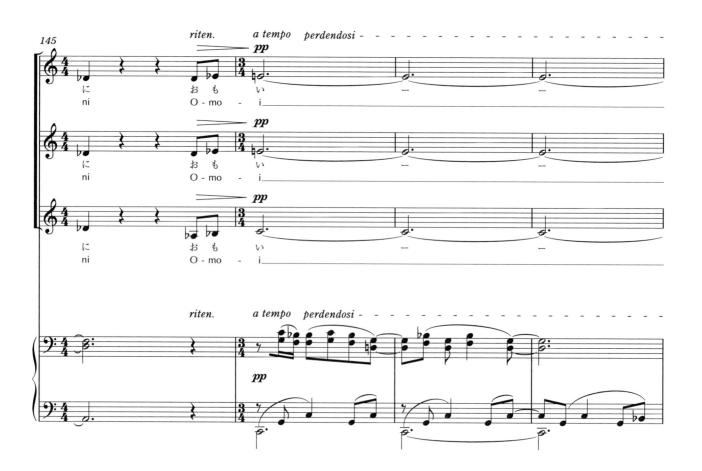

ほほえみ
Hohoemi
Smile

谷川俊太郎 作詩
Words by Shuntaro TANIKAWA
松下　耕 作曲
Composed by Ko MATSUSHITA

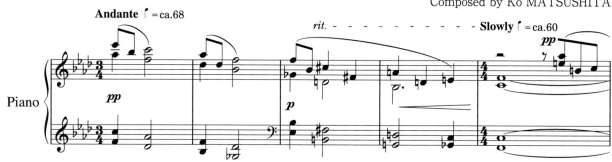
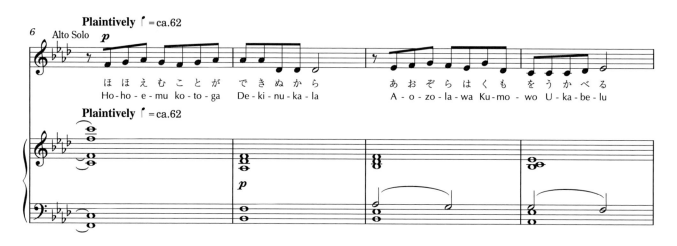
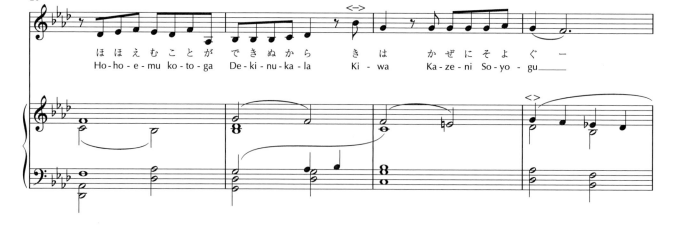
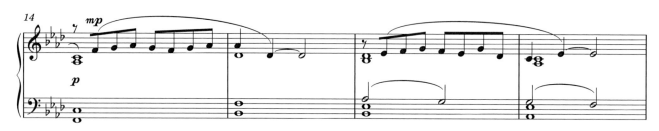

© Copyright 2006 by edition KAWAI, Tokyo, Japan. International Copyright Secured, All Rights Reserved.

楽譜・音楽書等出版物を複写・複製することは法律により禁じられております。

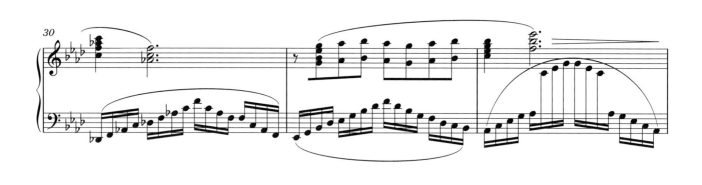
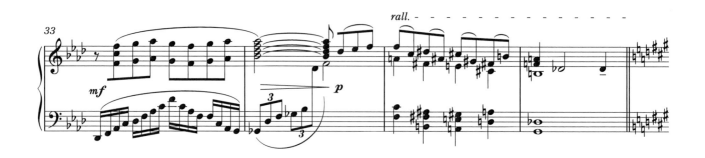

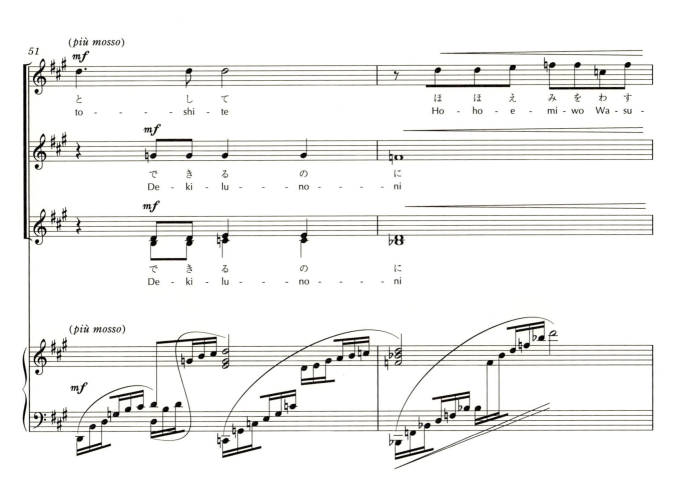

48

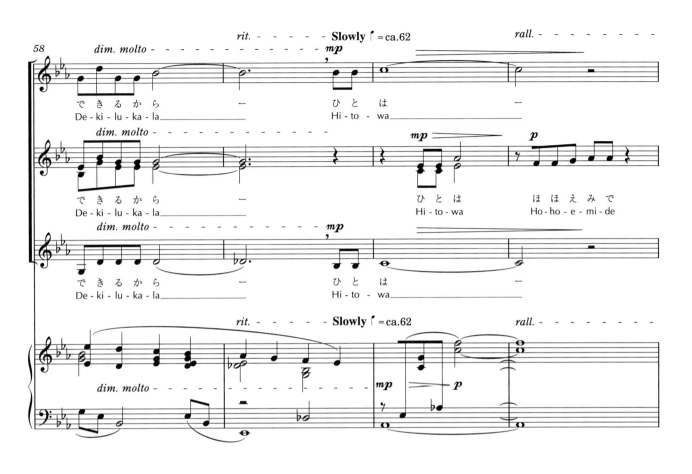
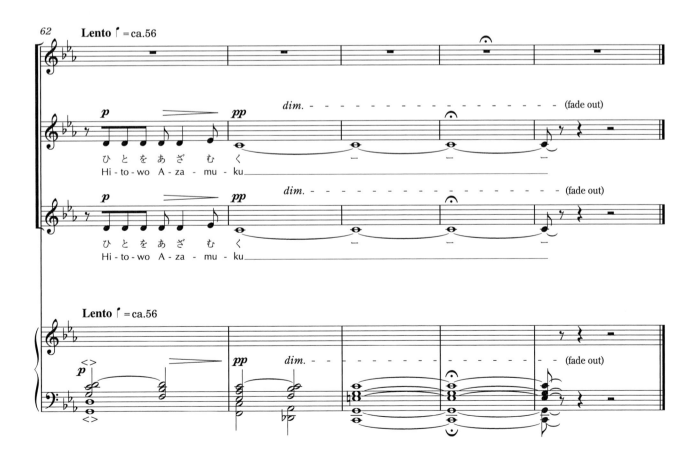

今年

Kotoshi

This Year

谷川俊太郎 作詩
Words by Shuntaro TANIKAWA
松下　耕 作曲
Composed by Ko MATSUSHITA

© Copyright 2006 by edition KAWAI, Tokyo, Japan. International Copyright Secured, All Rights Reserved.
楽譜・音楽書等出版物を複写・複製することは法律により禁じられております。

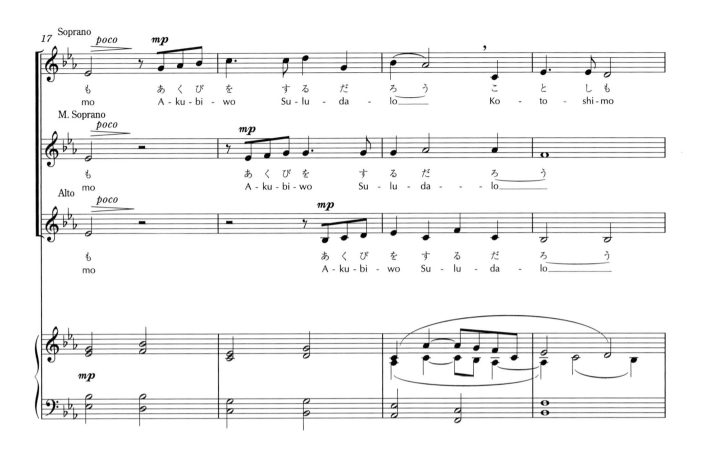

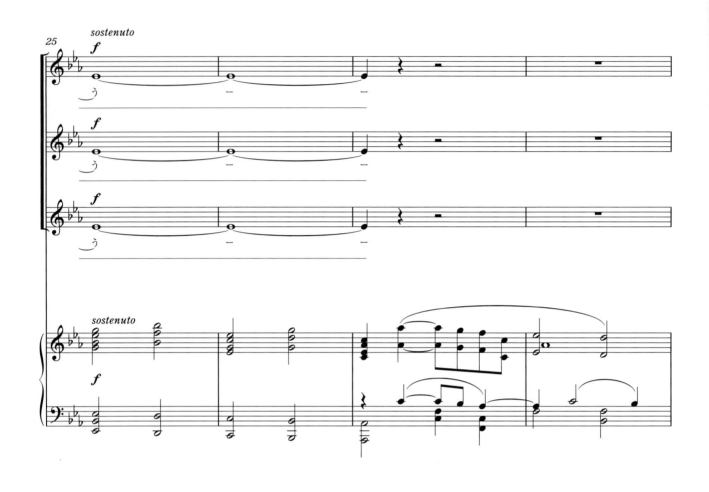

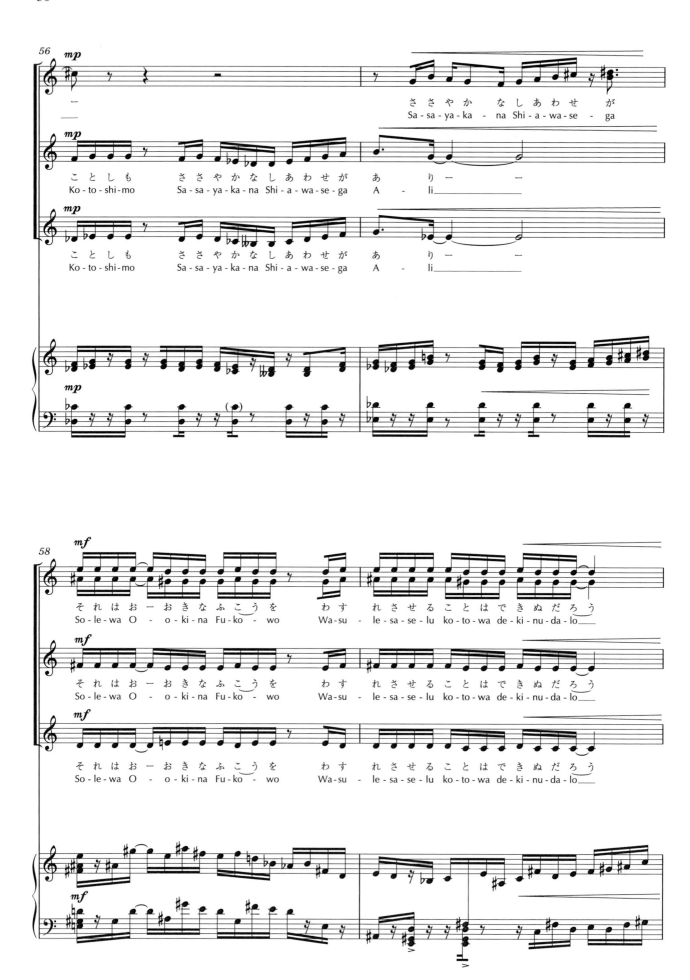

★ このC音はオプションです。C音を演奏しなくても構いません。
また、C音のかわりにB♭音で演奏しても構いません。
These C notes are options, in addition, you can play B♭ instead of C.

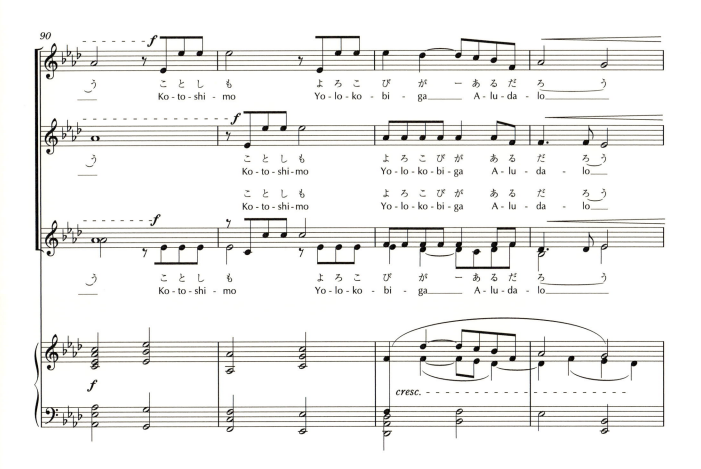

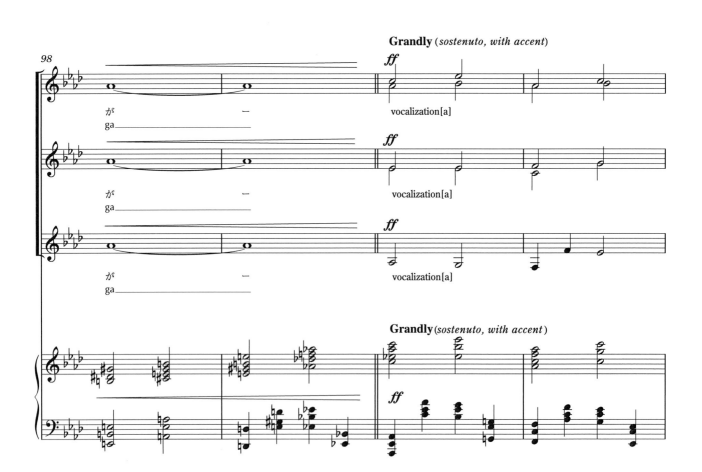

64

無伴奏版

は る

谷川俊太郎＝作詩
松 下　耕＝作曲

Spring

〔A cappella version〕

この星の上で　　谷川俊太郎

On our Planet　　Shuntaro Tanikawa
Translated by William I. Elliott and Kazuo Kawamura

はる　（「二十億光年の孤独」より）

はなをこえて
しろいくもが
くもをこえて
ふかいそらが

はなをこえ
くもをこえ
そらをこえ
わたしはいつまでものぼってゆける

はるのひととき
わたしはかみさまと
しずかなはなしをした

Spring

A dab of white cloud
over the cherry-blossoms
and beyond the cloud
a deep sky.

Over the blossoms,
beyond the cloud,
beyond the sky.
I can climb forever.

One moment of a spring day
I had a quiet talk
with a god.

Two Billion Light-Years of Solitude

地球の客　（「真っ白でいるよりも」より）

躾の悪い子どものように
ろくな挨拶もせず
青空の扉をあけ
大地の座敷に上がりこんだ

私たち　草の客
木々の客
鳥たちの客
水の客

したり顔で
出された御馳走に
舌つづみを打ち
景色を讃めたたえ

いつの間にか
主人になったつもり
文明の
なんという無作法

Guests of the Earth

Like spoiled children
we opened the door of the blue sky
and climbed into Earth's parlor
without giving proper greetings.

We are guests of grass,
of trees,
of birds
and of water.

When the feast is offered
we smack our lips
smugly
and praise the scenery.

We feel we have become, without knowing it,
their master.
Civilization is
unspeakably rude.

だがもう立ち去るには
遅すぎる
死は育むから
新しいいのちを

私たちの死後の朝
その朝の
鳥たちのさえずり
波の響き

遠い歌声
風のそよぎ
聞こえるだろうか
いま

But it's too late
to go elsewhere,
because death fosters
new life.

On the morning
of our death –
the morning songs of birds,
waves crashing,

distant voices singing,
leaves rustling in the wind –
Can you in this moment
hear them?

Better than Pure White

おべんとうの歌　（「うつむく青年」より）

魔法壜のお茶が
ちっともさめていないことに
何度でも感激するのだ
白いごはんの中から
梅干が顔を出す瞬間に
いつもスリルを覚えるのだ
ゆで卵のからが
きれいにくるりとむけると
手柄でもたてた気になるのだ
　（大切な薬みたいに
　　包んである塩）
キャラメルなどというものを
口に含むのを許されるのは
いい年をした大人にとって
こんな時だけ
奇蹟の時
おべんとうの時
空が青いということに
突然馬鹿か天才のように
夢中になってしまうのだ
小鳥の声が聞こえるといって
オペラの幕が開くみたいに
しーんとするのだ
そしてびっくりする
自分がどんな小さなものに
幸せを感じているかを知って
そして少し腹を立てる
あんまり簡単に
幸せになった自分に

A Song of Lunch

I am always amazed
that the tea in the thermos
stays perfectly hot.
I'm always thrilled at the moment
the pickled plum shows its face
from within the white rice.
When the shell slips cleanly away
from the hard boiled egg
I feel I've achieved something.
(The salt is wrapped in paper
like an important medicine.)
It's only when we eat
this kind of lunch
that we adults have a chance
to eat caramel candy.
A momentary miracle,
this lunch time.
We are suddenly carried away
like either fools or geniuses
by the blueness of the sky.
As the little birds begin chirping
we fall silent,
as at the beginning of an opera.
And I am surprised to know
that even the smallest of things
fills me with happiness.
And I feel a little cross
with myself
for being made happy so easily.

—あそこでは
そうあの廃坑になった町では
おべんとうのある子は
おべんとうを食べていた
そして
おべんとうのない子は
風の強い校庭で
黙ってぶらんこにのっていた
その短い記事と写真を
何故こんなにはっきり
記憶しているのだろう
どうすることもできぬ
くやしさが
泉のように湧きあがる
どうやってわかちあうのか
幸せを
どうやってわかちあうのか
不幸を

手の中の一個のおむすびは
地球のように
重い

—There,
yes, in that abandoned mining town
children who had lunch
were eating lunch,
and
children who had none
were silently swinging
on the playground in a strong wind.
Why do I so clearly recall that short newspaper article
and the photograph?
A sense of personal helplessness
wells up
like a spring.
How on earth can we share
happiness?
How on earth can we share
unhappiness?

The single rice ball I hold in my hand
is as heavy
as the earth.

A Young Man With Down-Cast Eyes

ほほえみ （「空に小鳥がいなくなった日」より）

ほほえむことができぬから
青空は雲を浮べる
ほほえむことができぬから
木は風にそよぐ

ほほえむことができぬから
犬は尾をふり—だが人は
ほほえむことができるのに
時としてほほえみを忘れ

ほほえむことができるから
ほほえみで人をあざむく

Smile

Because it cannot smile
the blue sky carries clouds.
Because they cannot smile
trees sough in the wind.

Because they cannot smile
dogs wag their tails. But people,
though they can smile,
sometimes forget to,

and because they can smile,
smiling, they deceive one another.

The Day the Birds Disappeared from the Sky

今年 (「祈らなくていいのか」より)

涙があるだろう
今年も
涙ながらの歌があるだろう
固めたこぶしがあるだろう
大笑いがあるだろう今年も
あくびをするだろう
今年も
短い旅に出るだろう
そして帰ってくるだろう
農夫は野に
数学者は書斎に
眠れぬ夜があるだろう
だが愛するだろう
今年も
自分より小さなものを
自分を超えて大きなものを

くだらぬことに喜ぶだろう
今年も
ささやかな幸せがあり
それは大きな不幸を
忘れさせることはできぬだろう
けれど娘は背が伸びるだろう
そして樹も
御飯のおいしい日があるだろう
新しい靴を一足買うだろう
決心はにぶるだろう今年も
しかし去年とちがうだろうほんの少し
今年は

地平は遠く果てないだろう
宇宙へと大きなロケットはのぼり
子等は駆けてゆくだろう
今年も歓びがあるだろう
生きてゆくかぎり
いなむことのできぬ希望が

This Year

There may be tears
this year, too.
There may be songs with tears
and a clenched fist.
There may also be loud laughter this year.
We may yawn
this year, too.
We may set out on a short trip
and may come back—
the farmer to his field,
the mathematician to his study.
There may be sleepless nights;
but we may love
this year, too,
things smaller than ourselves,
things larger than and beyond ourselves.

This year, too,
we may find delight in trifling things,
and there may be some modest happiness
which might not allow us to forget
a great unhappiness.
But our daughters may grow taller,
as may trees.
Days there may be of delicious meals.
We may buy a new pair of shoes.
Our resolve may weaken, this year, too.
but things may be a bit different from last year,
this year.

The horizon may recede further and further,
a giant rocket may ascend into space
and children may go on running.
This year, too, there may be joy.
There may be undeniable hope,
as long as we keep on living.

Don't We Need to Pray?

女声合唱とピアノのための この星の上で 谷川俊太郎 作詩／松下 耕 作曲

●発行所＝カワイ出版（株式会社 全音楽譜出版社 カワイ出版部）
〒161-0034 東京都新宿区上落合 2-13-3　TEL 03-3227-6286／FAX 03-3227-6296
出版情報 https://www.editionkawai.jp/
●楽譜浄書＝NHKビジネスクリエイト　●印刷・製本＝平河工業社

ⓒ 2006 by edition KAWAI. Assigned 2017 to Zen-On Music Co., Ltd.
●楽譜・音楽書等出版物を複写・複製することは法律により禁じられております。落丁・乱丁本はお取り替え致します。
本書のデザインや仕様は予告なく変更される場合がございます。
ISBN978-4-7609-1623-8

2006 年 8 月 1 日　第 1 刷発行
2025 年 6 月 1 日　第 43 刷発行